# Wisconsin Barn Quilt
## Coloring Book Three
### John H. Lettau

# Barn Quilts of Shawano County, Wisconsin

### Cover Barn Quilts

Castor & Pollux
Six Windows of Sunshine
Marigold Garden
Joseph's Coat

# *Shawano County Wisconsin Barn Quilt Project*

A drive through Shawano County, in Northern Wisconsin, is very colorful today because more than 325 brilliant "barn blocks," called barn quilts, are displayed on barns and other structures throughout the rural area that surrounds the city of Shawano. Four typical Shawano County barn quilts located in the Shawano area are pictured above...Stars & Triangles, King Solomon's Puzzle, Wheel of Fortune, and Patchwork Star.

The Shawano County Barn Quilt Project was started by writer/photographer Jim Leuenberger in 2010. In June 2010 Jim proposed the idea to local 4H clubs as possible club service projects. Since then, clubs, individuals, families, organizations, and businesses have sponsored and painted barn blocks. Individual barn owners have supported the project by having quilt blocks mounted on barns and/or other farm structures. The barn quilt trend continues to grow today because of the interest and talents of Jim and his wife Irene. The Shawano project hopes to...encourage the preservation of Shawano County's historic barns, promote tourism for Shawano County, and provide opportunities for groups and individuals to sponsor and paint barn quilts as a community service project.

### Objective s of Barn Quilt Projects

Barn quilt trails and projects help to promote and celebrate the unique agricultural heritage and history through the visual combination of rural barns and quilt patterns. Barns are vital to the economic well being of the rural community and surrounding area. Handmade quilts provide warmth, beauty and an outlet for individual and group artistic expression.

### *What is a Barn Quilt?*

A barn quilt is made by painting a quilt pattern on two 4' by 8' sheets of ¾ inch MDO plywood. Two coats of primer are applied to both sides and edges. After the pattern is drawn out, Frog (painters) tape is used to outline the various sections of the pattern. Three coats of each color, or more, are applied, with each coat being allowed to dry overnight. After the quilt is finished it is allowed to cure for at least two weeks before it is put upon the barn.

Making a barn quilt allows individuals and volunteer groups the opportunity to create and paint their own quilt square. The design that is chosen may represent a family pattern from a loved quilt or perhaps a new pattern meaningful to the individual creator(s).

### Shawano County Barn Quilt Project Information
Books-Maps-Information-Tours
Shawano County Chamber of Commerce
1623 South Main Street Shawano, Wisconsin 54166
715-524-2139805 235 8528 www.shawanocounty,com

# Shawano County Wisconsin Barn Quilts

| | | |
|---|---|---|
| Milk Way Star | Hwy 160 | Pulaski |
| Weathervane Pinwheel | Mavis Rd | Wittenberg |
| Patchwork Stars | Porter Rd | Shawano |
| 4H is Fun | Green Bay St | Bonduel |
| On Eagles Wings | Maplewood Rd | Birnamwood |
| Yellow Chick | County Rd D | Birnamwood |
| American Pride | County Rd E | Shawano |
| Our Nine | Green Valley Rd | Pulaski |
| Old Glory | Birch Rd | Bonduel |
| Stars and Triangles | Stony Hill Rd | Marion |
| Patchwork Heart | Maple Ave | Shawano |
| King Solomon's Puzzle | Trout Lane | Birnamwwood |
| Passing Time | County Rd E | Shawano |
| Snowy Morning | School House Rd | Wittenberg |
| Blazing Star | County Rd F | Zachow |
| Apple Tree | County Rd A | Gresham |
| Compass Star | Hwy 47-55 | Shawano |
| Tall Ship | River Bank Rd | Clintonville |
| 1904 Star | Spruce Rd | Wittenberg |
| Special Memories | Henselin Rd | Tigerton |
| Wheel of Fortune | Maplewood Rd | Birnamwood |
| Quarter Horse Star | River Rd | Wittenberg |
| Diamond Star | Krueger Rd | Caroline |
| Four X Quilt | White Clay Lake Dr | Cecil |
| Star Shine | Broadway Rd | Bonduel |
| Susie's Choice | Wheeler Ave | Eland |
| Marigold Garden | County Rd G | Leopolis |
| Cross of Peace | County Rd SS | Tigerton |
| Six Windows of Sunshine | County Rd E | Shawano |
| American Hunter | Belle Plaine Ave | Shawano |
| Square Diamond | Main Laney Dr | Pulaski |
| Flowering Nine Patch | County Rd G | Leopolis |
| Double Star Flower | Range Line Rd | Shawano |
| Arrow Crown | Belle Plaine Ave | Shawano |
| Castle Garden | Lake Rd | Birnamwood |
| Building the Stars | County Rd S | Pulaski |
| Morning Star | Green Valley Rd | Krakow |
| Rural Connections | County Rd V | Cecil |
| Joeph's Coat | Ash Rd | Shawano |
| Always in Tune | County Rd K | Shawano |
| Let Freedom Ring | County Trunk CC | Shawano |
| Game Farm | J&H Rd | Shiocton |
| Mosaic Squares | Hwy 22 | Shawano |
| Victorian Star | County Trunk CC | Shawano |
| The Wishing Horse | County Rd C | Krakow |
| Wisconsin | Hwy 22 | Shawano |
| Norwegian Cross | Hwy 156 | Shiocton |
| Castor and Pollux | Wilson Creek Lane | Wittenberg |
| Never Forget | Hwy 22 | Cecil |
| Family Traditions | Deering Lane | Cecil |

# *Milky Way Star*

## *Shawano County Wisconsin Barn Quilts*

*Barn Location*
*Hwy 160*
*Pulaski, Wisconsin*

# Wisconsin Barn Quilt Milky Way Star

# Weathervane Pinwheel

## Shawano County Wisconsin Barn Quilts

Barn Location
Mavis Rd..
Wittenberg, Wisconsin

# Wisconsin Barn Quilt Weathervane Pinwheel

# Patchwork Stars
## Shawano County Wisconsin Barn Quilts

*Barn Location
Porter Rd..
Shawano, Wisconsin*

# Wisconsin Barn Quilt Patchwork Stars

# 4H is Fun
## Shawano County Wisconsin Barn Quilts

Barn Location
West Green Bay St
Bonduel, Wisconsin

# Wisconsin Barn Quilt 4 H is Fun

# On Eagles Wings
## Shawano County Wisconsin Barn Quilts

Barn Location
Maplewood Rd
Birnamwood, Wisconsin

# Wisconsin Barn Quilt On Eagles Wings

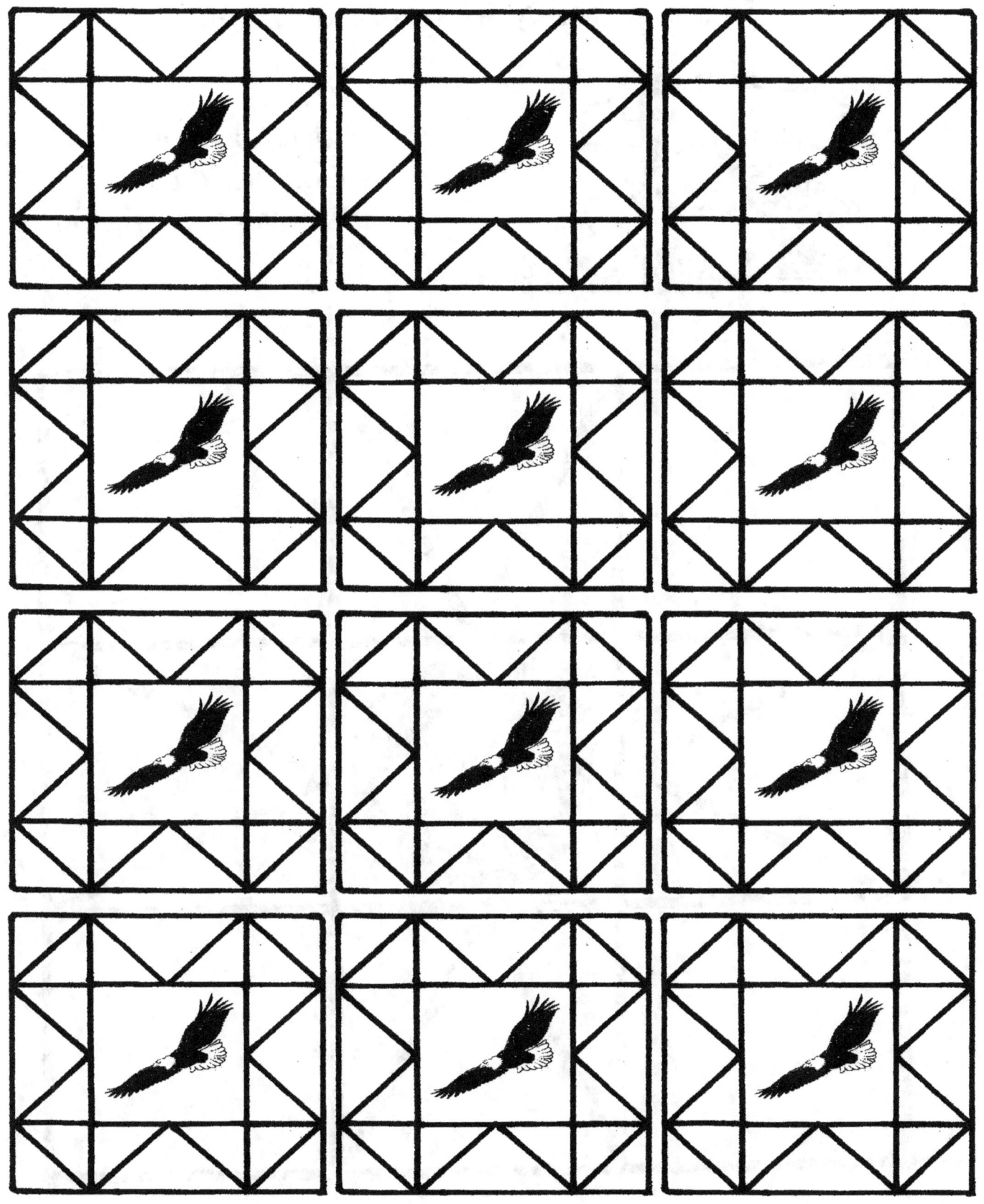

# Yellow Chick
## Shawano County Wisconsin Barn Quilts

*Barn Location*
*County Rd D*
*Birnamwood, Wisconsin*

# Wisconsin Barn Quilt Yellow Chick

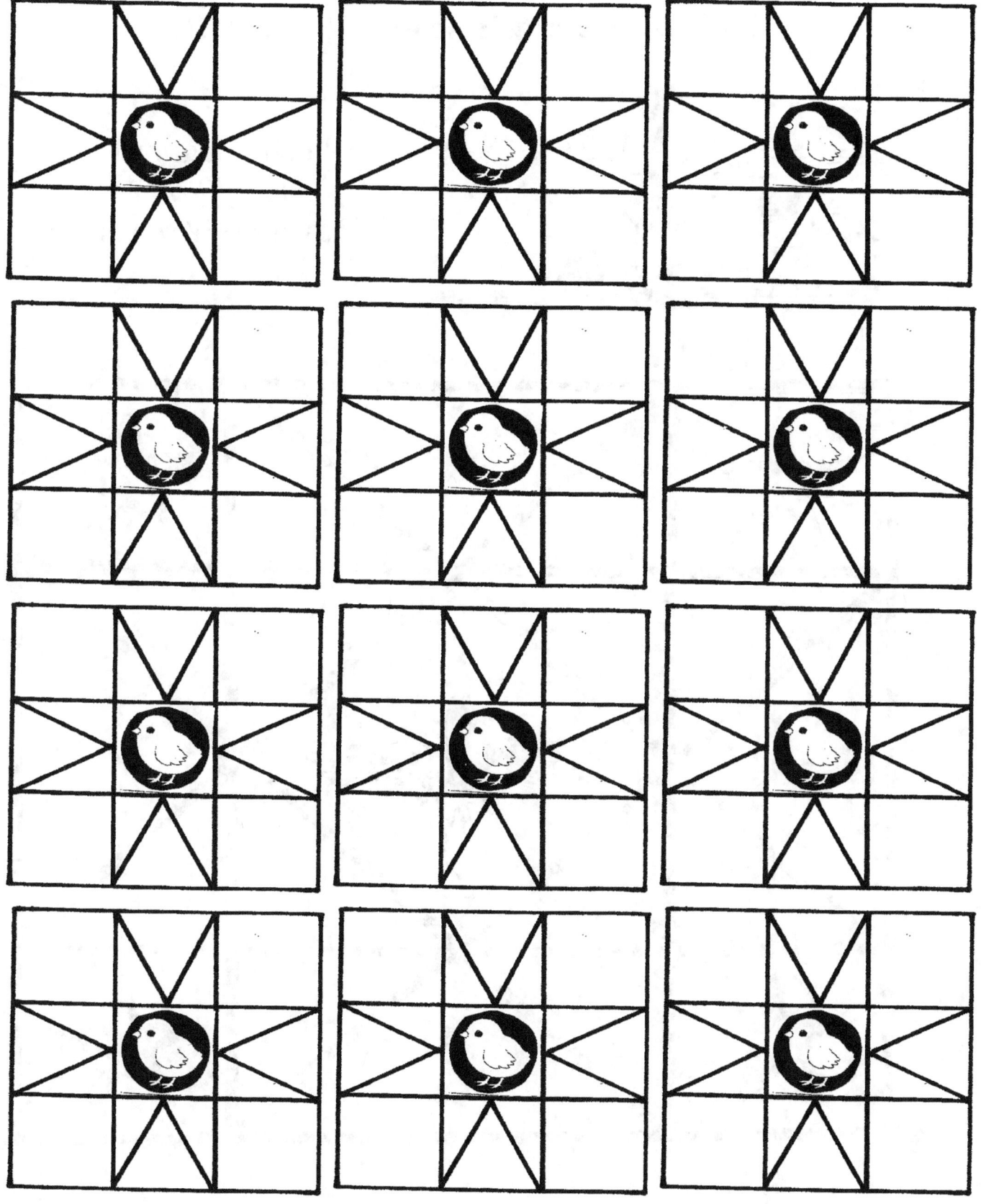

# American Pride
## Shawano County Wisconsin Barn Quilts

*Barn Location*
*County Rd E*
*Shawano, Wisconsin*

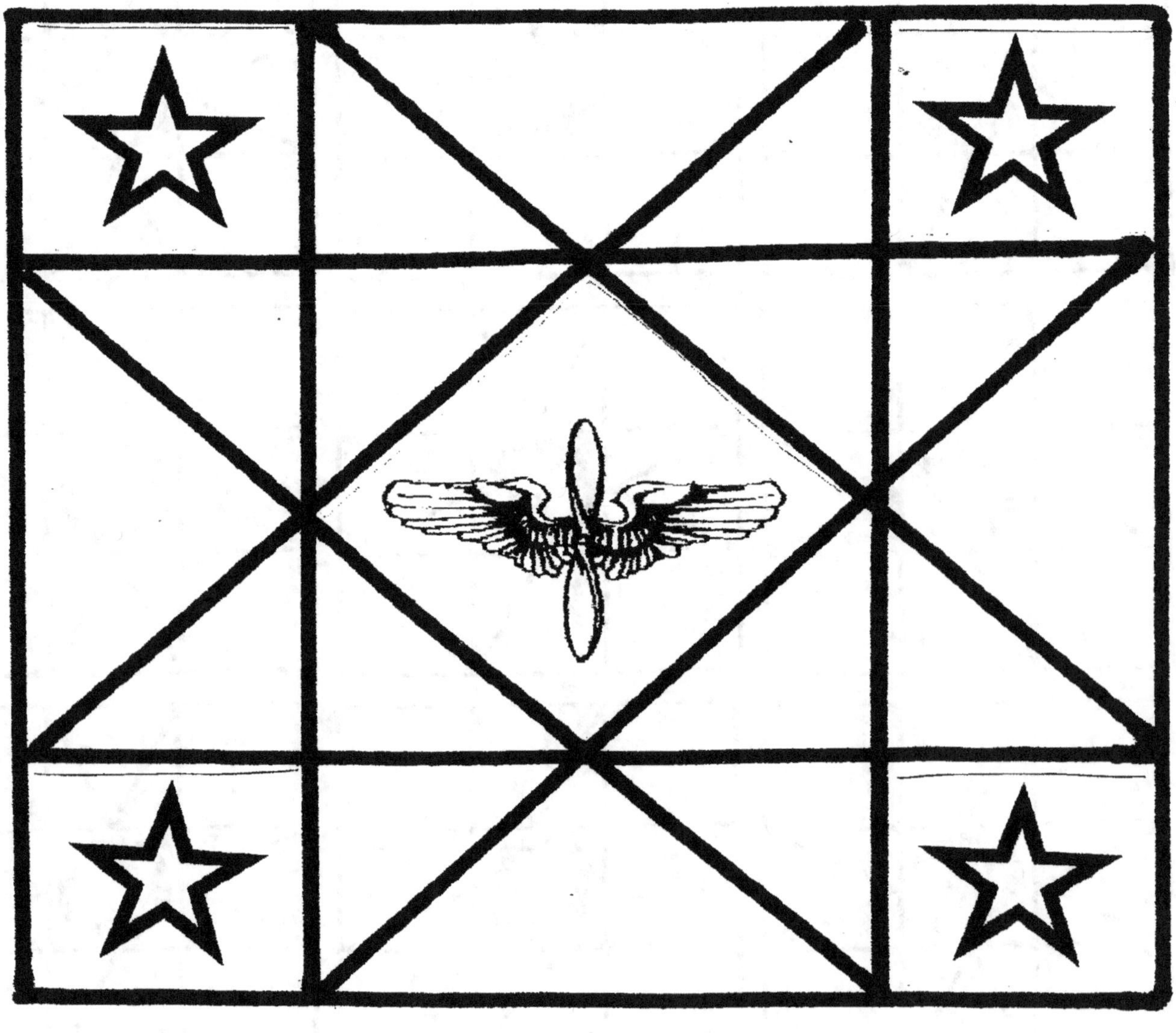

# Wisconsin Barn Quilt American Pride

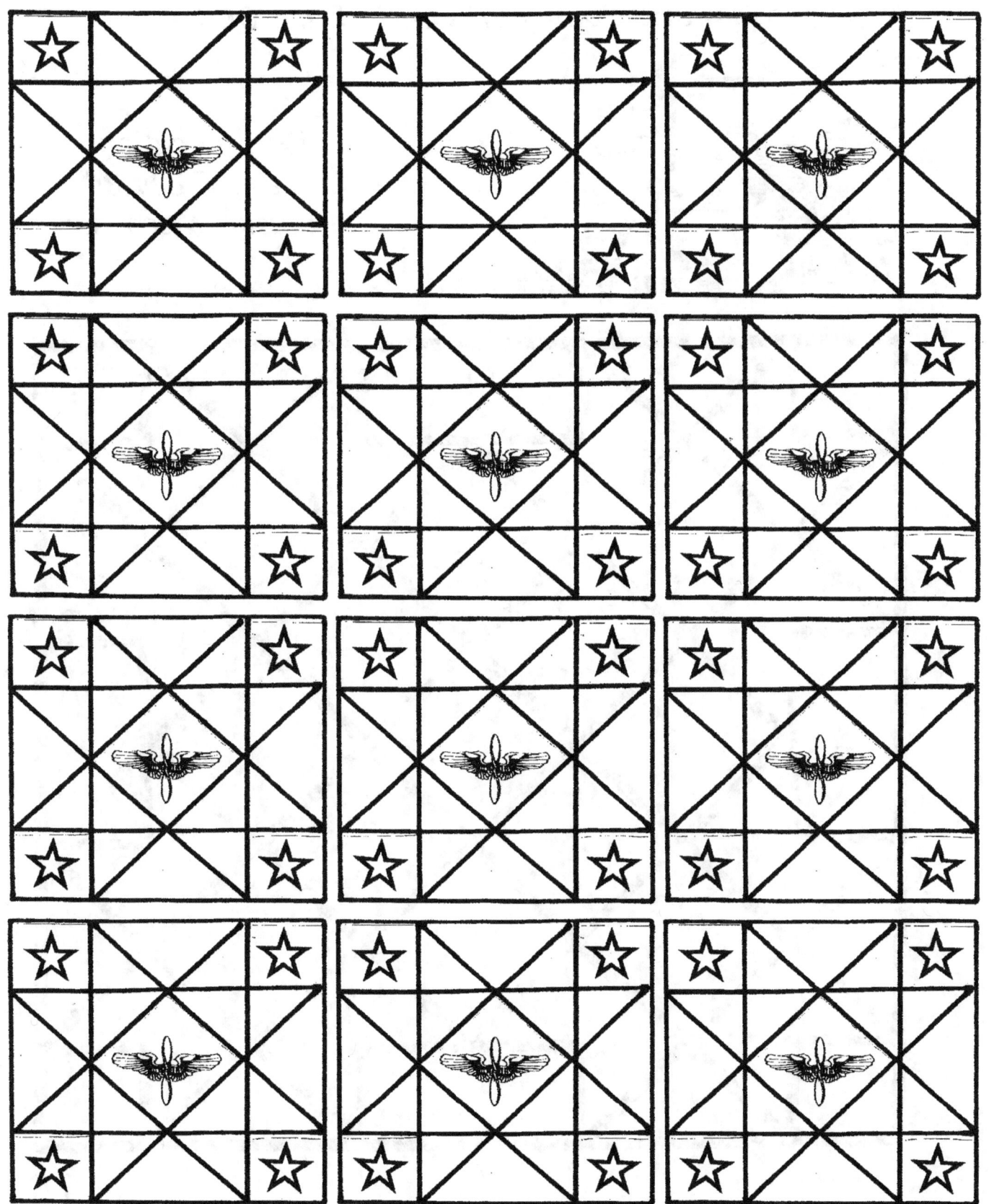

# Our Nine

## Shawano County Wisconsin Barn Quilts

**Barn Location**
**Green Valley Rd**
**Pulaski, Wisconsin**

# Wisconsin Barn Quilt Our Nine

# Old Glory
## Shawano County Wisconsin Barn Quilts

Barn Location
Birch Rd
Bonduel, Wisconsin

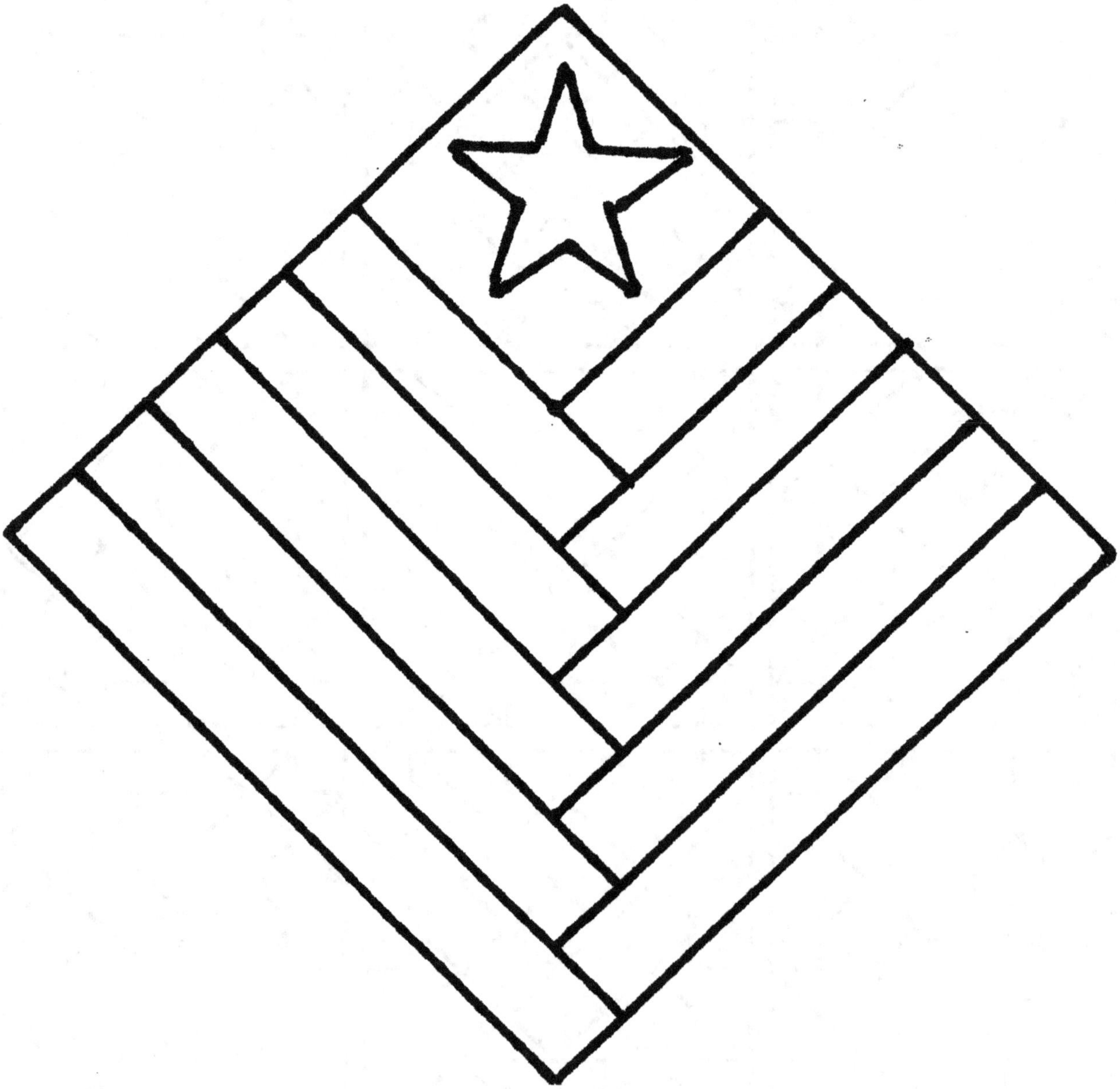

# Wisconsin Barn Quilt Old Glory

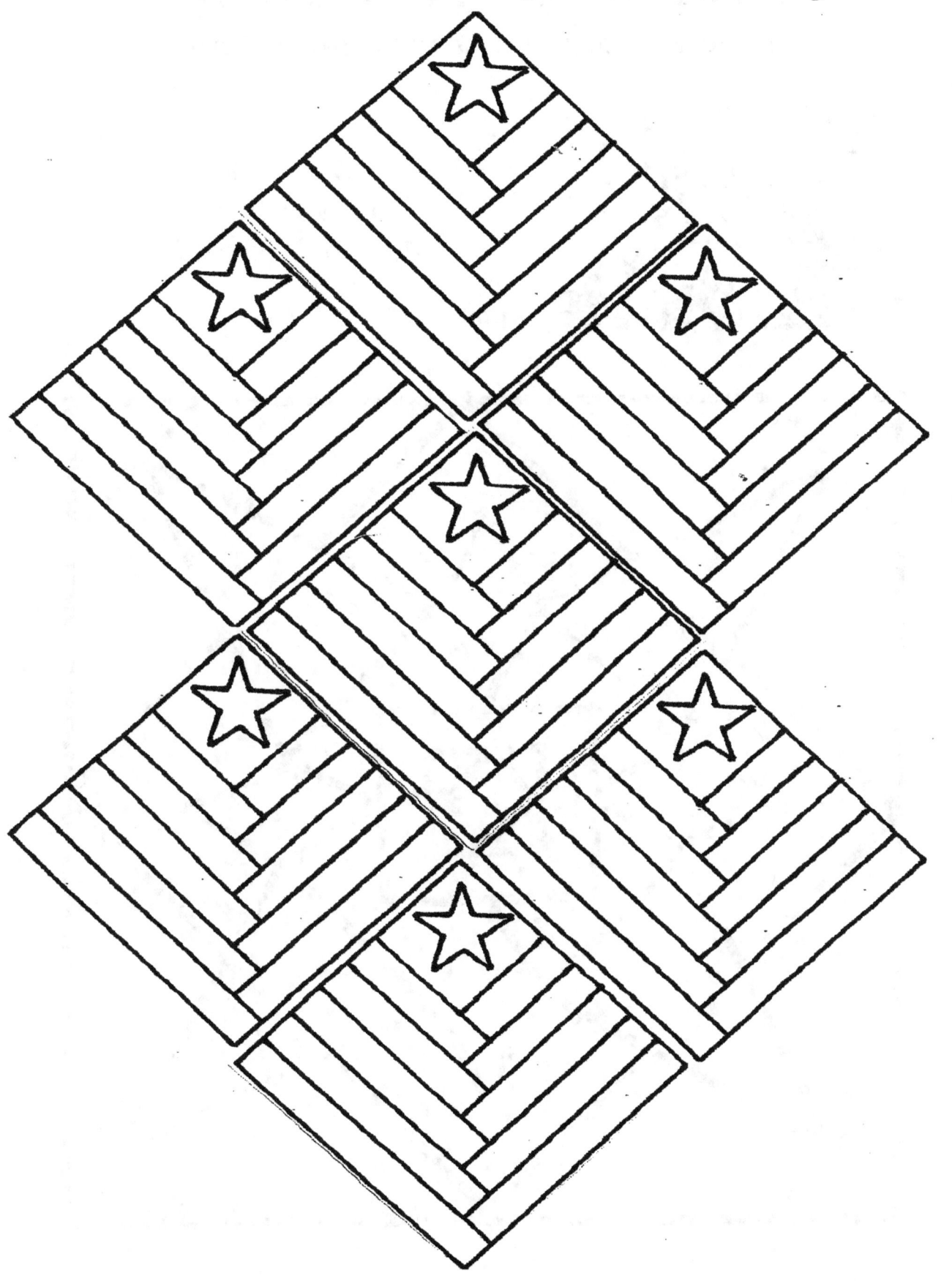

# Stars and Triangles
## Shawano County Wisconsin Barn Quilts

*Barn Location*
*Stony Hill Rd*
*Marion, Wisconsin*

# Wisconsin Barn Quilt Stars and Triangles

# Patchwork Heart

## Shawano County Wisconsin Barn Quilts

Barn Location
Maple Ave
Shawano, Wisconsin

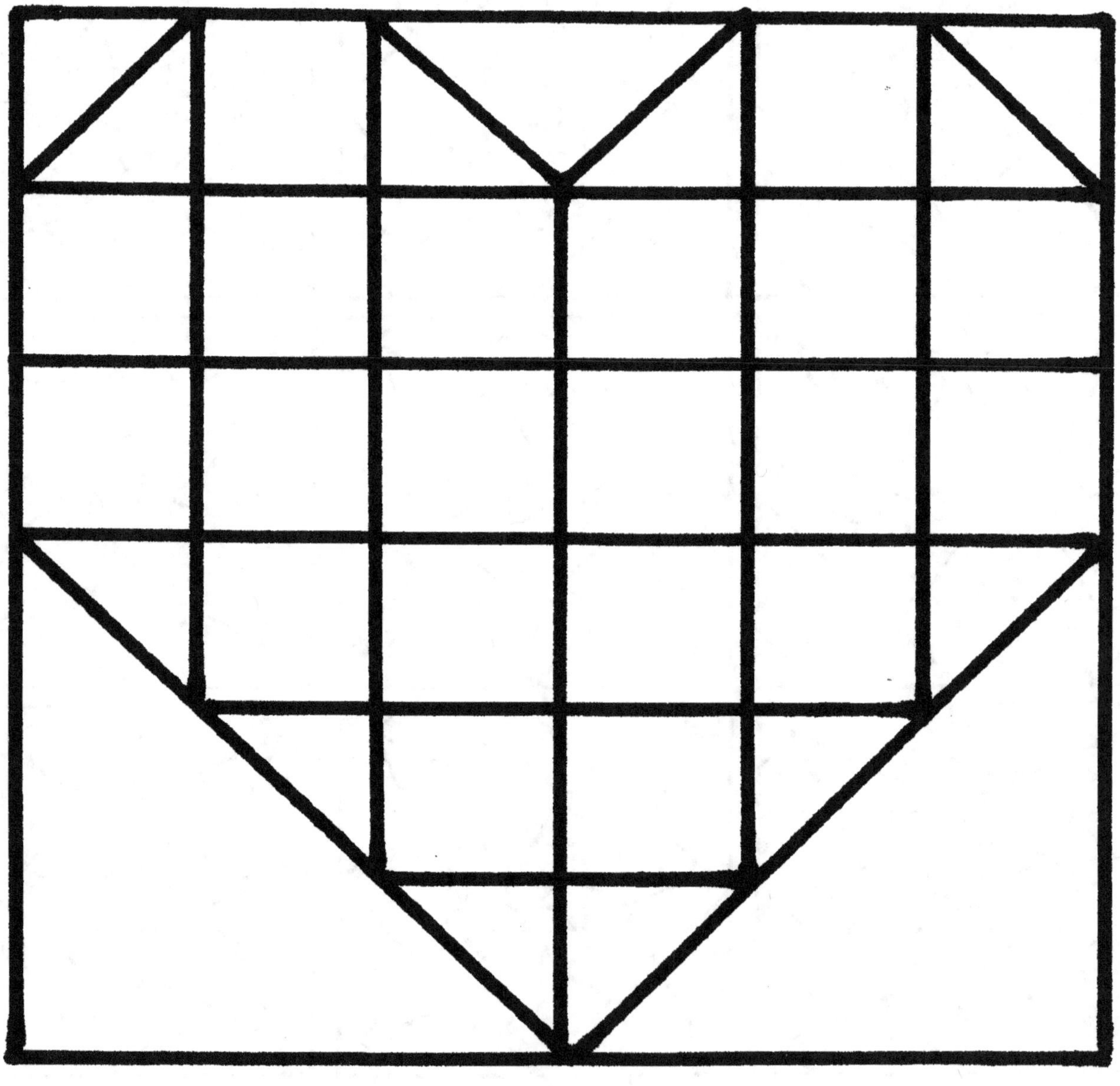

# Wisconsin Barn Quilt Patchwork Heart

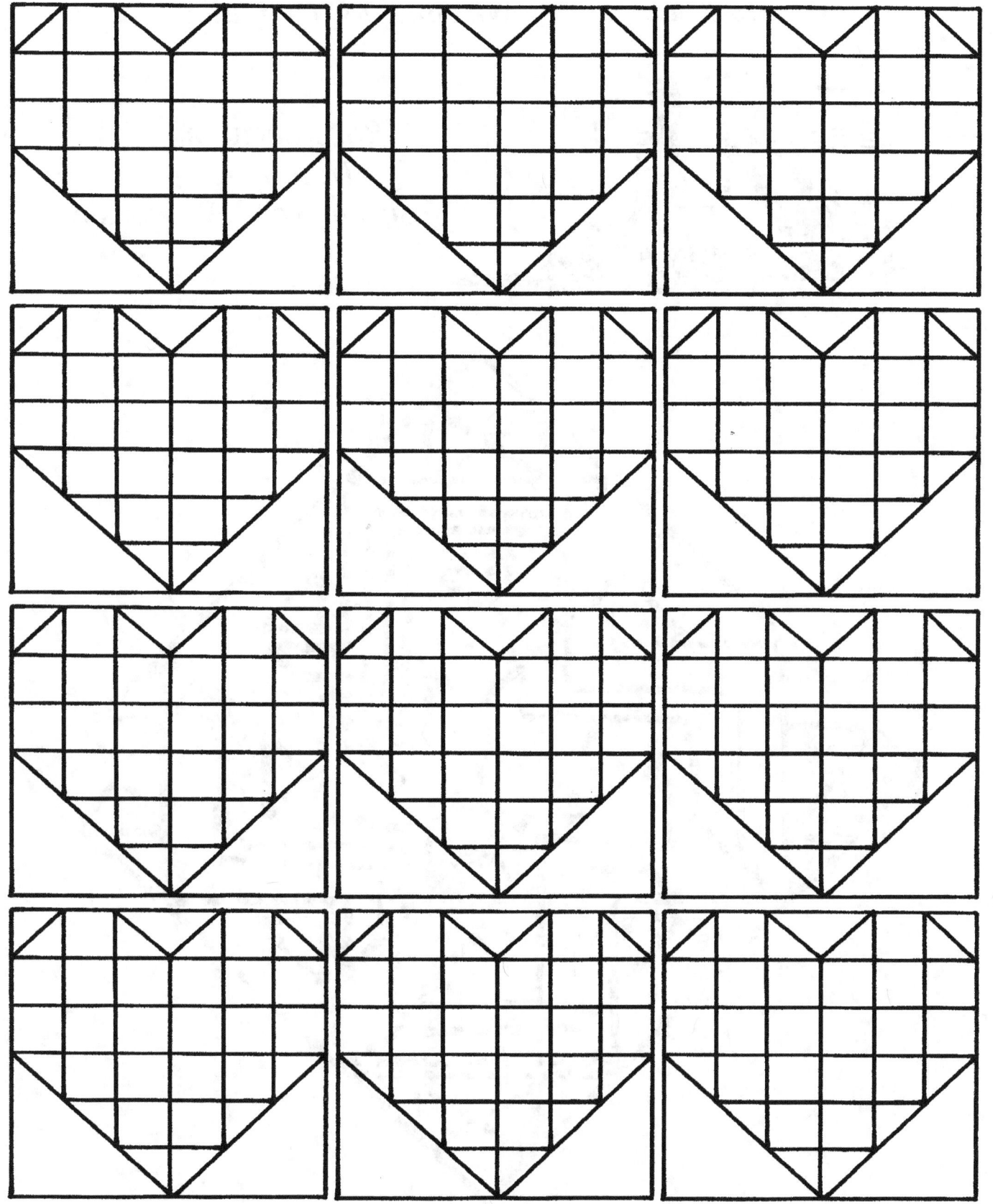

# King Solomon's Puzzle

## Shawano County Wisconsin Barn Quilts

*Barn Location*
*Trout Lane*
*Birnamwood, Wisconsin*

# Wisconsin Barn Quilt King Solomon's Puzzle

# Passing Time

## *Shawano County Wisconsin Barn Quilts*

*Barn Location*
*County Rd E*
*Shawano, Wisconsin*

# Wisconsin Barn Quilt Passing Time

# Snowy Morning

## Shawano County Wisconsin Barn Quilts

*Barn Location*
*School House Rd*
*Wittenberg, Wisconsin*

# Wisconsin Barn Quilt Snowy Morning

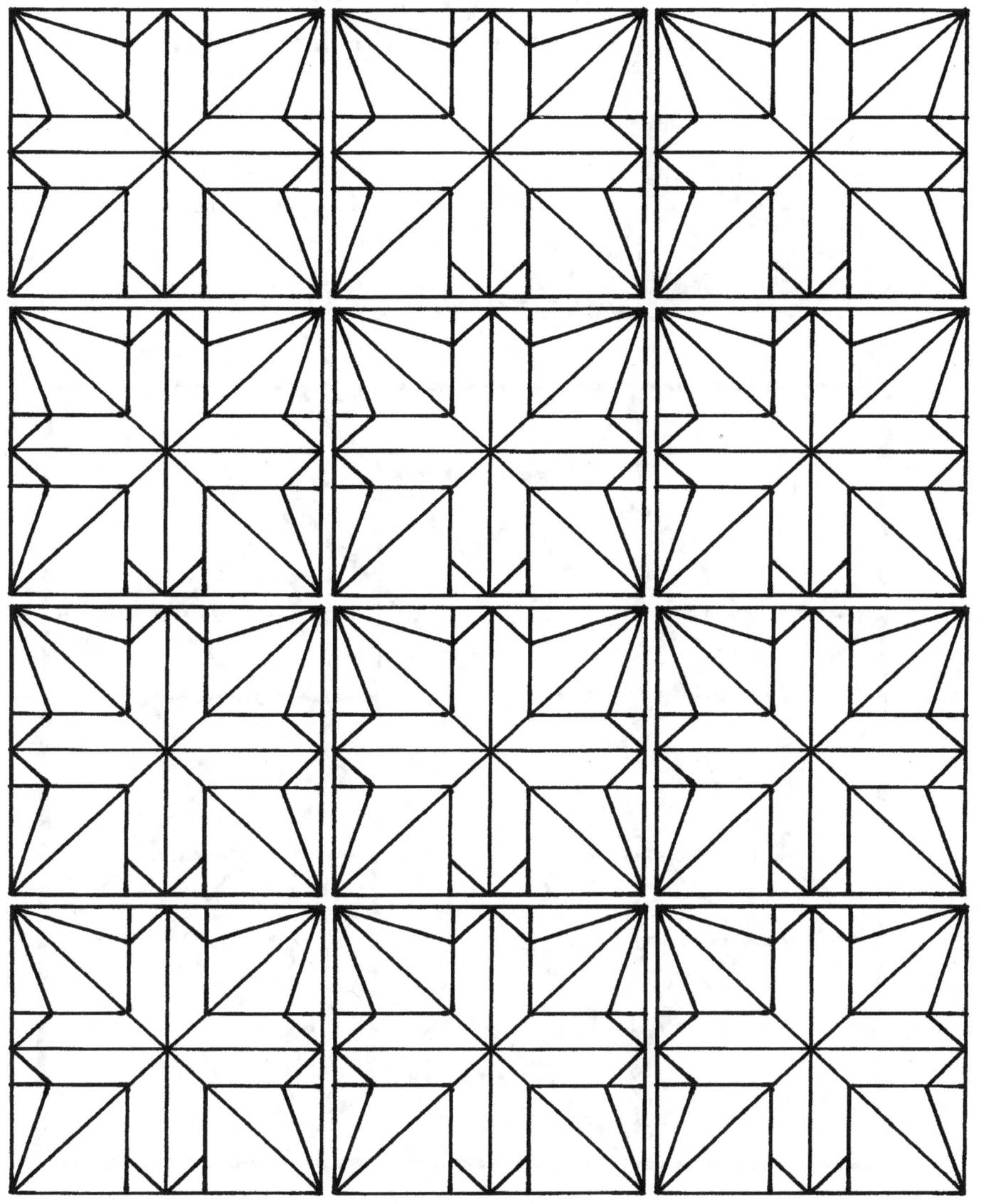

# Blazing Star

## Shawano County Wisconsin Barn Quilts

*Barn Location*
*County Rd F*
*Zachow, Wisconsin*

# Wisconsin Barn Quilt Blazing Star

# Apple Tree
## Shawano County Wisconsin Barn Quilts

*Barn Location*
*County Rd A*
*Gresham, Wisconsin*

# Wisconsin Barn Quilt Apple Tree

# *Compass Star*

## *Shawano County Wisconsin Barn Quilts*

*Barn Location
State Hwy 47-55
Shawano, Wisconsin*

# Wisconsin Barn Quilt Compass Star

# Tall Ship
## Shawano County Wisconsin Barn Quilts

*Barn Location*
*River Bank Rd*
*Clintonville, Wisconsin*

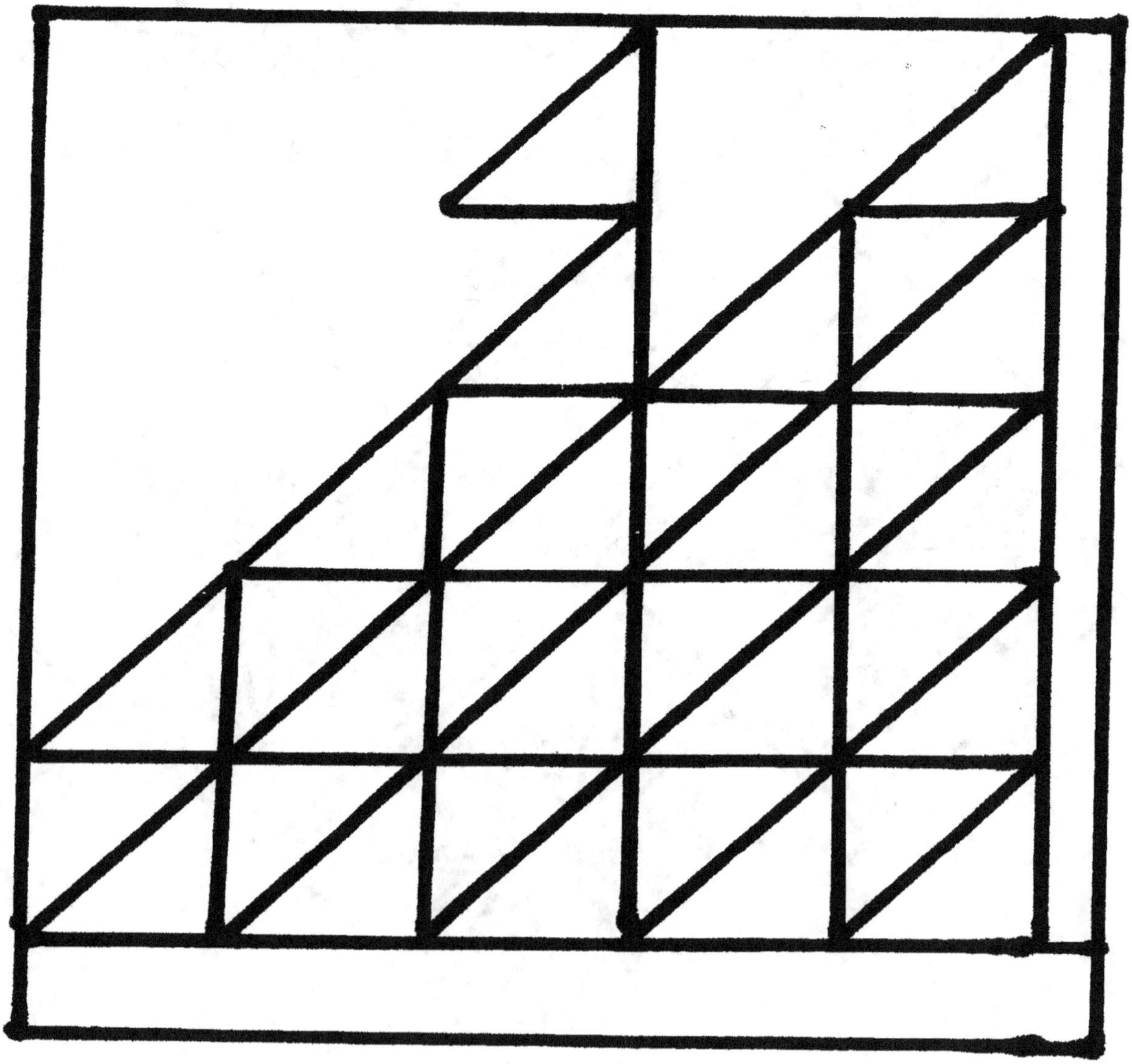

# Wisconsin Barn Quilt Tall Ship

# 1904 Star

### Shawano County Wisconsin Barn Quilts

*Barn Location*
*Spruce Rd*
*Wittenberg, Wisconsin*

# Wisconsin Barn Quilt 1904 Star

# Special Memories
## Shawano County Wisconsin Barn Quilts

Barn Location
Henselin Rd
Tigerton, Wisconsin

# Wisconsin Barn Quilt Special Memories

# Wheel of Fortune

## Shawano County Wisconsin Barn Quilts

Barn Location
Maplewood Rd
Birnamwood, Wisconsin

# Wisconsin Barn Quilt Wheel of Fortune

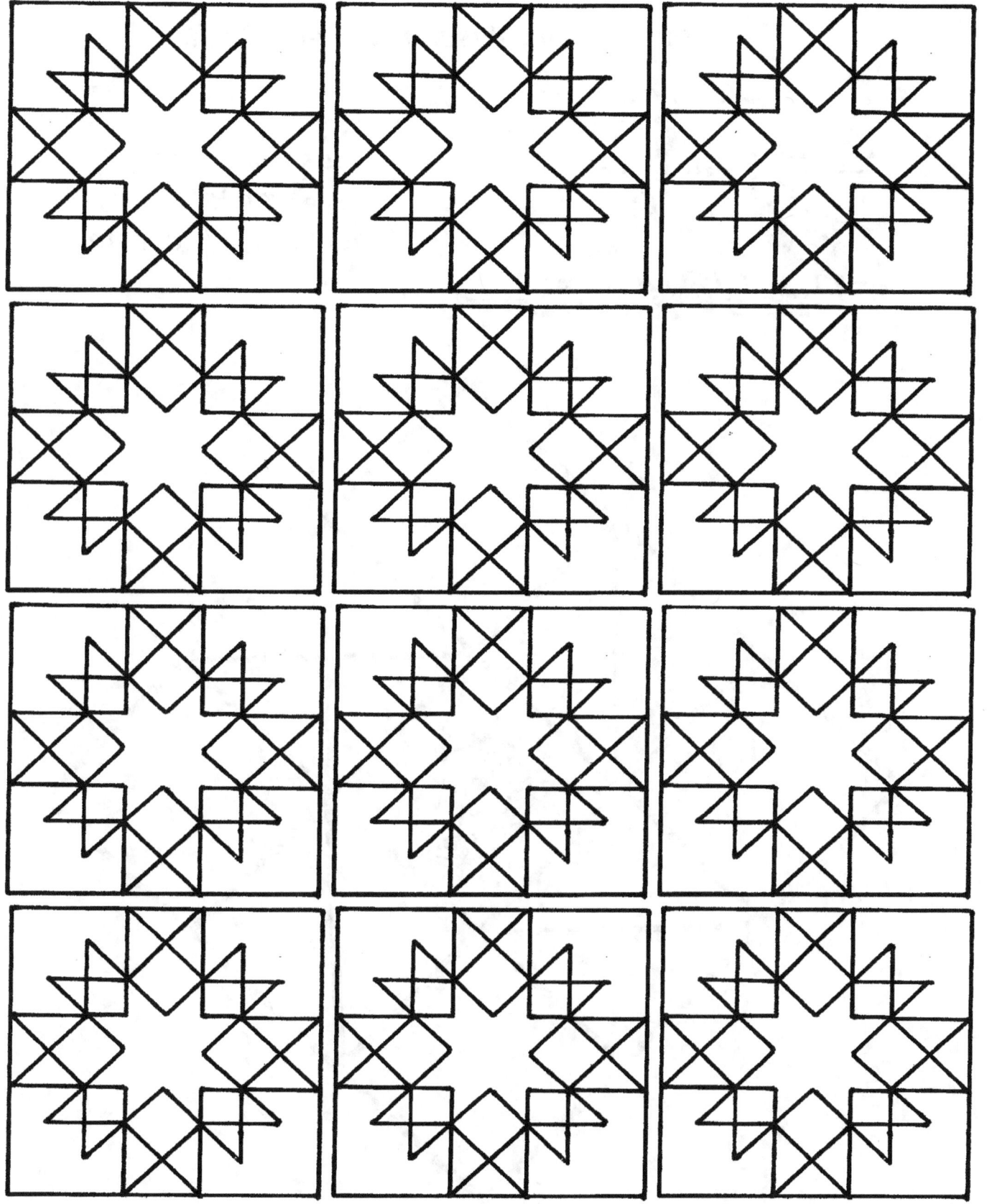

# Quarter Horse Star

## Shawano County Wisconsin Barn Quilts

**Barn Location**
*River Rd*
*Wittenberg, Wisconsin*

# Wisconsin Barn Quilt Quart Horse Star

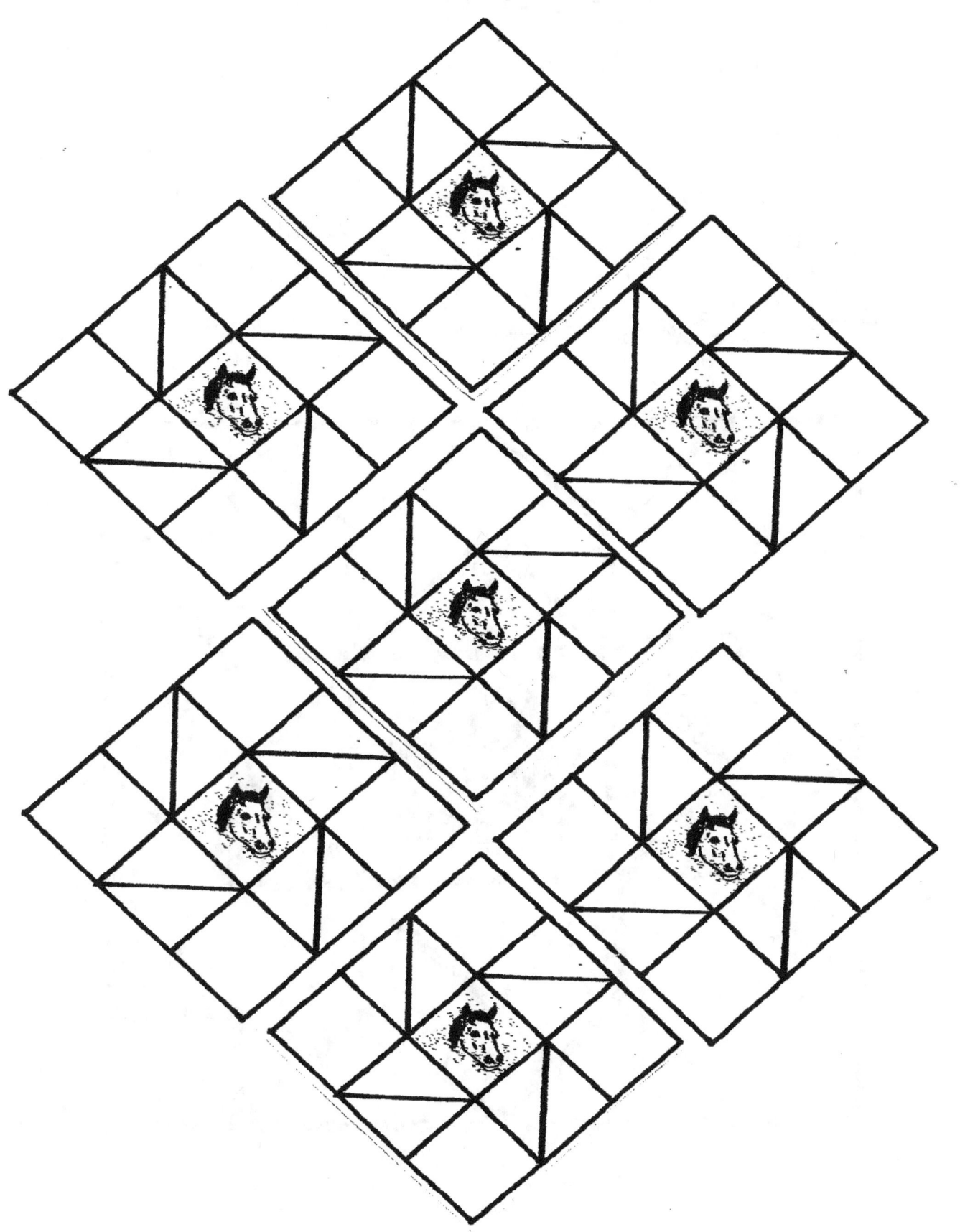

# Diamond Star

## Shawano County Wisconsin Barn Quilts

*Barn Location*
*Krueger Rd*
*Caroline, Wisconsin*

# Wisconsin Barn Quilt Diamond Star

# *Four X Quilt*

## *Shawano County Wisconsin Barn Quilts*

*Barn Location*
*White Clay Lake Dr*
*Cecil, Wisconsin*

**P**

# Wisconsin Barn Quilt Four X Quilt

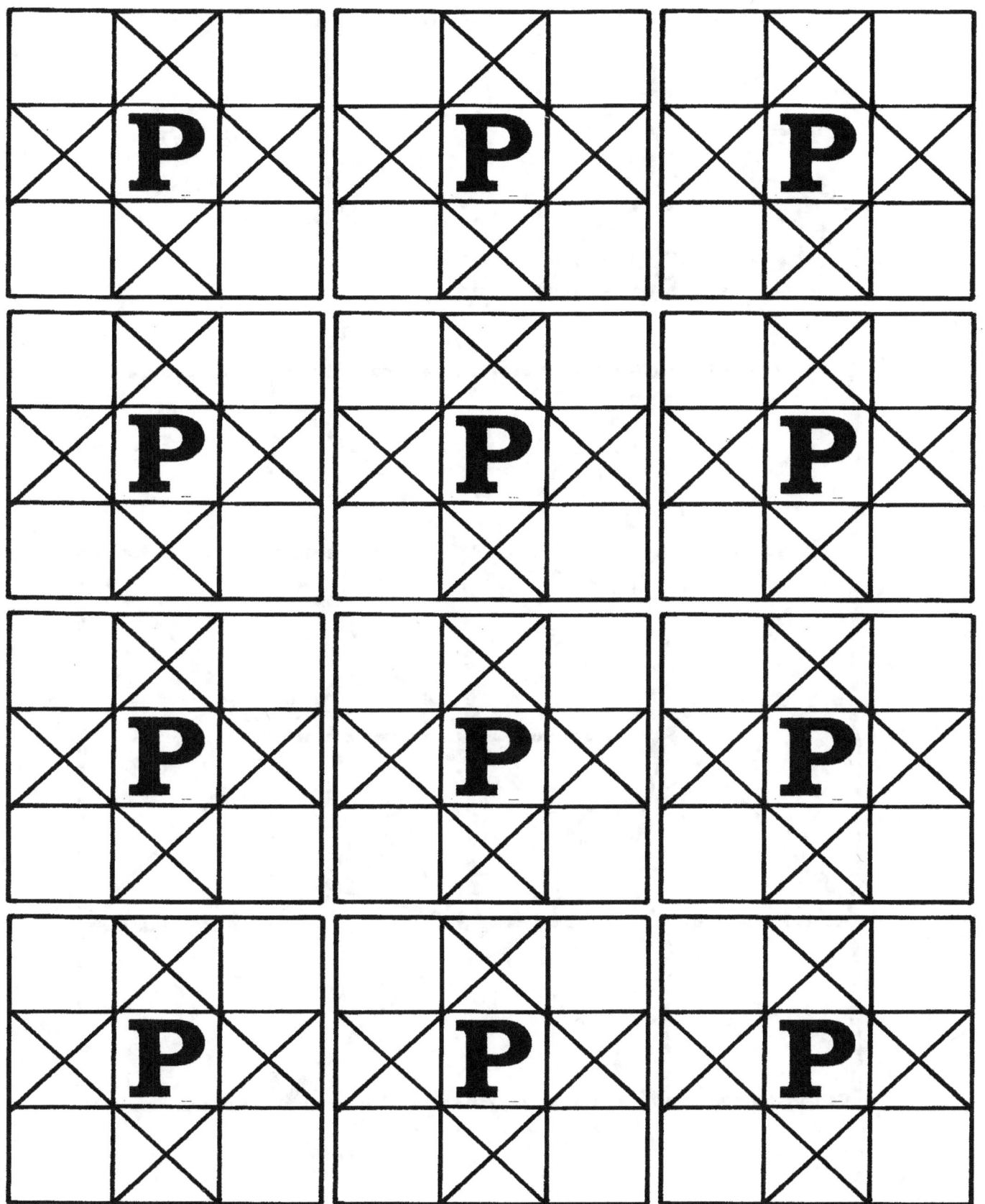

# Star Shine

## Shawano County Wisconsin Barn Quilts

*Barn Location*
*Broadway Rd*
*Bonduel, Wisconsin*

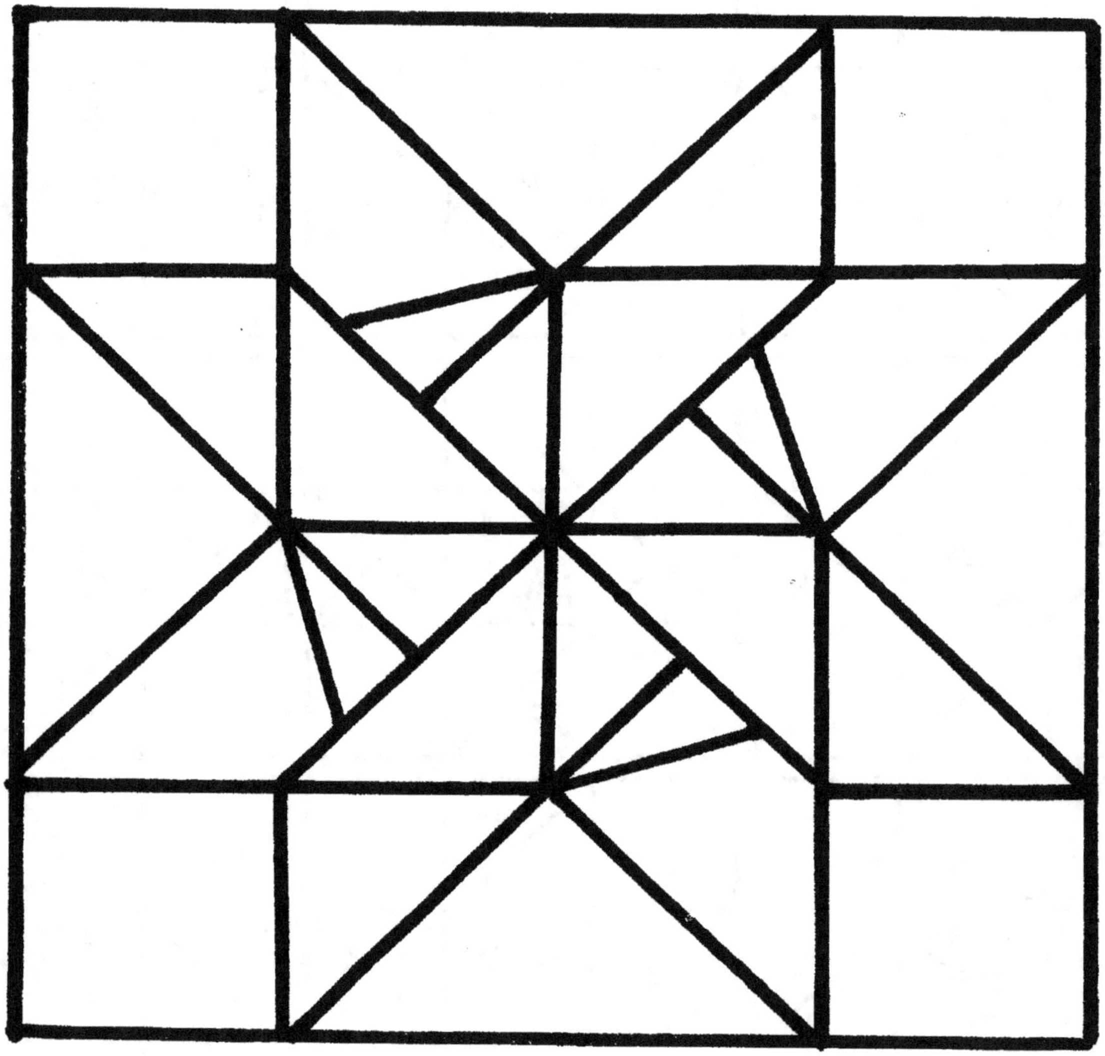

# Wisconsin Barn Quilt Star Shine

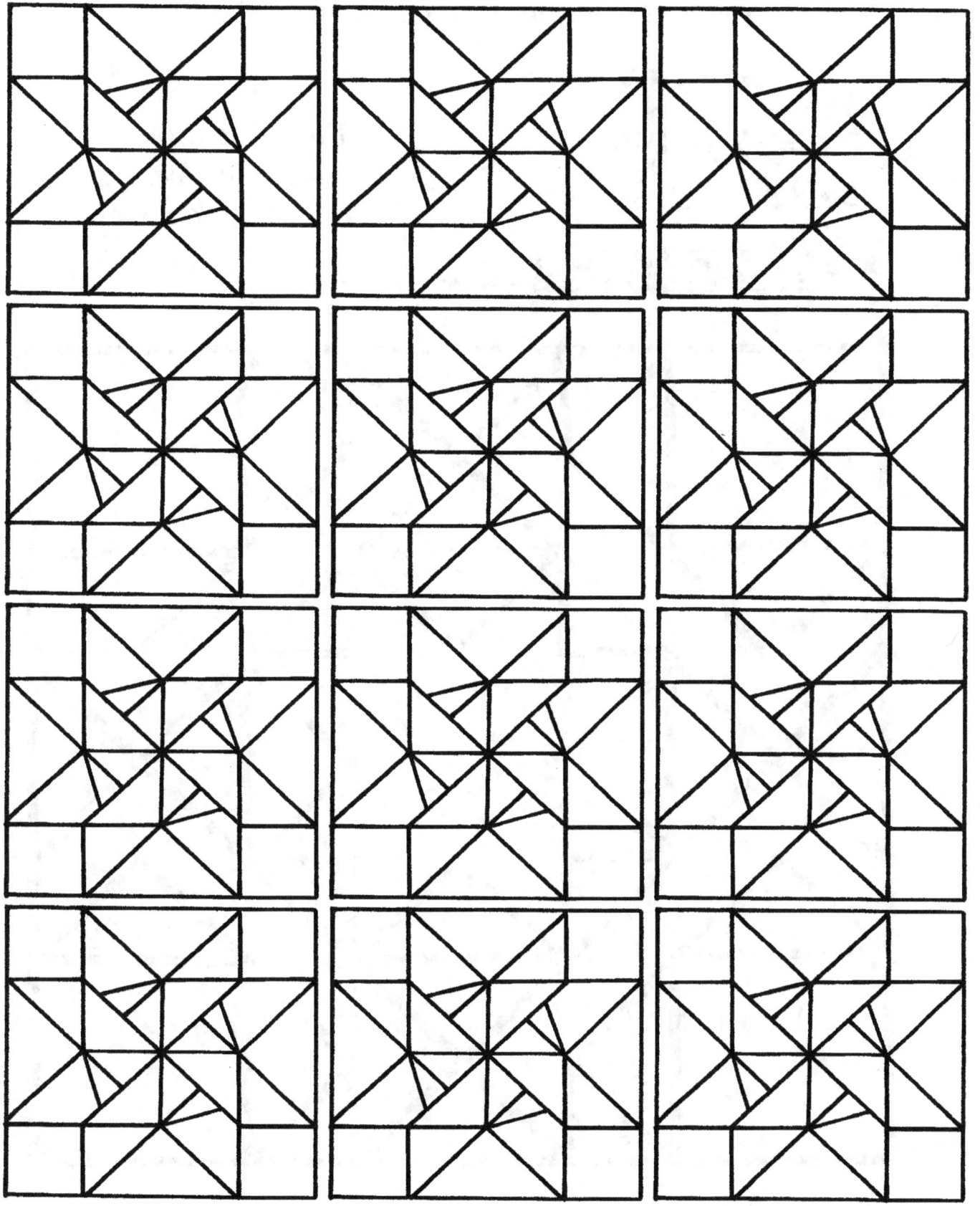

# Susie's Choice

## Shawano County Wisconsin Barn Quilts

*Barn Location*
*Wheeler Ave*
*Eland, Wisconsin*

# Wisconsin Barn Quilt Susie's Choice

# Marigold Garden
## Shawano County Wisconsin Barn Quilts

*Barn Location*
*County Rd G*
*Leopolis, Wisconsin*

# Wisconsin Barn Quilt Marigold Garden

# Cross of Peace
## Shawano County Wisconsin Barn Quilts

*Barn Location*
*County Rd SS*
*Tigerton, Wisconsin*

# Wisconsin Barn Quilt Cross of Peace

# Six Windows of Sunshine

## Shawano County Wisconsin Barn Quilts

*Barn Location*
*County Rd E*
*Shawano, Wisconsin*

# Wisconsin Barn Quilt Six Windows of Sunshine

# American Hunter

## Shawano County Wisconsin Barn Quilts

*Barn Location*
*Belle Plaine Ave*
*Shawano, Wisconsin*

# Wisconsin Barn Quilt American Hunter

# Square Diamond
### Shawano County Wisconsin Barn Quilts

*Barn Location*
*Main Laney Dr*
*Pulaski, Wisconsin*

# *Wisconsin Barn Quilt Square Diamond*

# Flowering Nine Patch

## Shawano County Wisconsin Barn Quilts

*Barn Location*
*County Rd G*
*Leopolis, Wisconsin*

# Wisconsin Barn Quilt Flowering Nine Patch

# Double Star Flower

## Shawano County Wisconsin Barn Quilts

*Barn Location*
*Range Line Rd*
*Shawano, Wisconsin*

# Wisconsin Barn Quilt Double Star Flower

# *Arrow Crown*

### *Shawano County Wisconsin Barn Quilts*

*Barn Location*
*Belle Plaine Ave*
*Shawano, Wisconsin*

# Wisconsin Barn Quilt Arrow Cross

# Castle Garden

## Shawano County Wisconsin Barn Quilts

*Barn Location*
*Lake Rd*
*Birnamwood, Wisconsin*

# Wisconsin Barn Quilt Castle Garden

# Building the Stars

## Shawano County Wisconsin Barn Quilts

*Barn Location*
*County Rd S*
*Pulaski, Wisconsin*

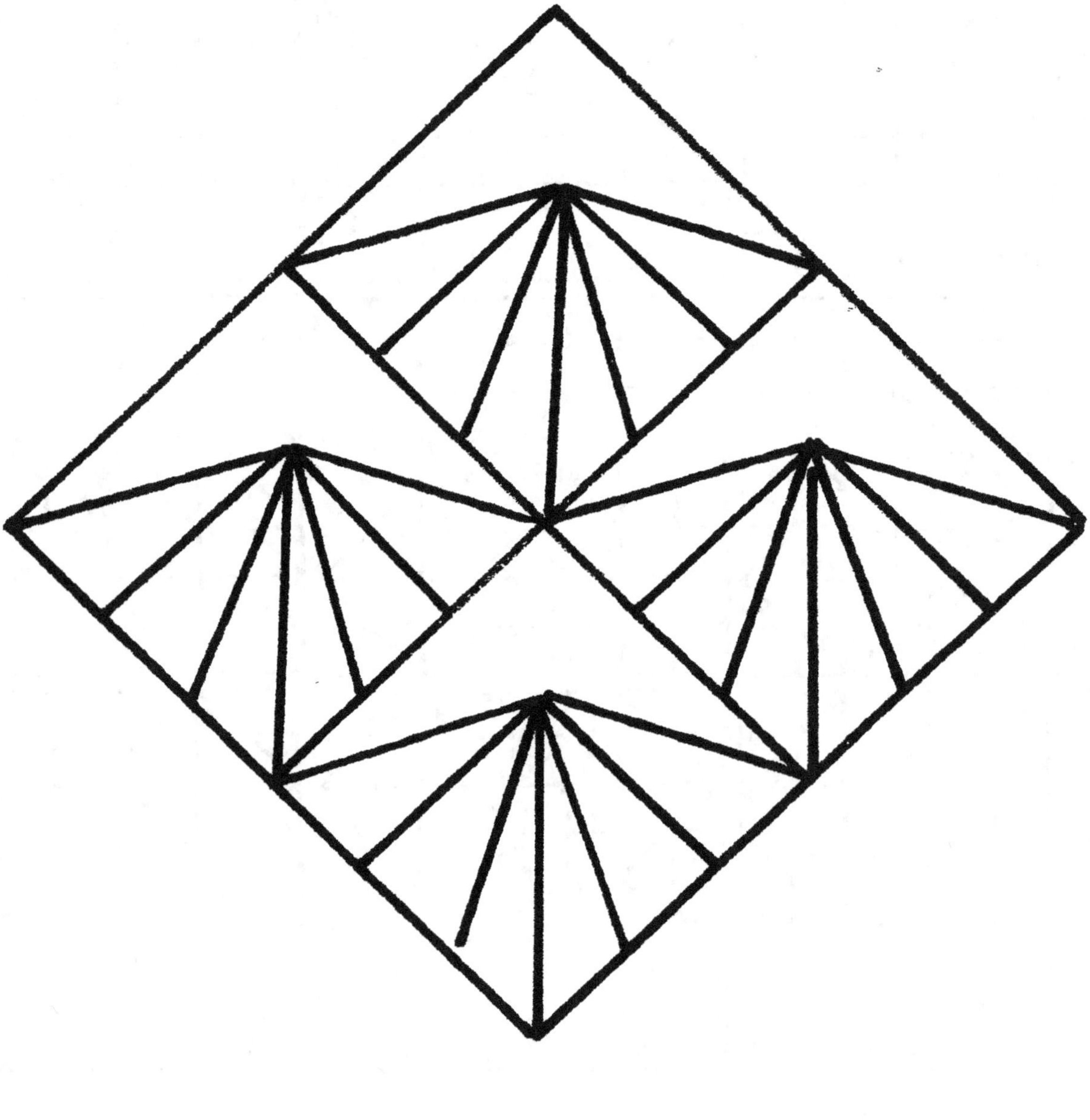

# Wisconsin Barn Quilt Building the Stars

# Morning Star
## Shawano County Wisconsin Barn Quilts

*Barn Location*
*Green Valley Rd*
*Krakow, Wisconsin*

# Wisconsin Barn Quilt Morning Star

# Rural Connections

## Shawano County Wisconsin Barn Quilts

*Barn Location*
*County Rd V*
*Cecil, Wisconsin*

# Wisconsin Barn Quilt Rural Connections

# Joseph's Coat
## Shawano County Wisconsin Barn Quilts

*Barn Location*
*Ash Rd*
*Shawano, Wisconsin*

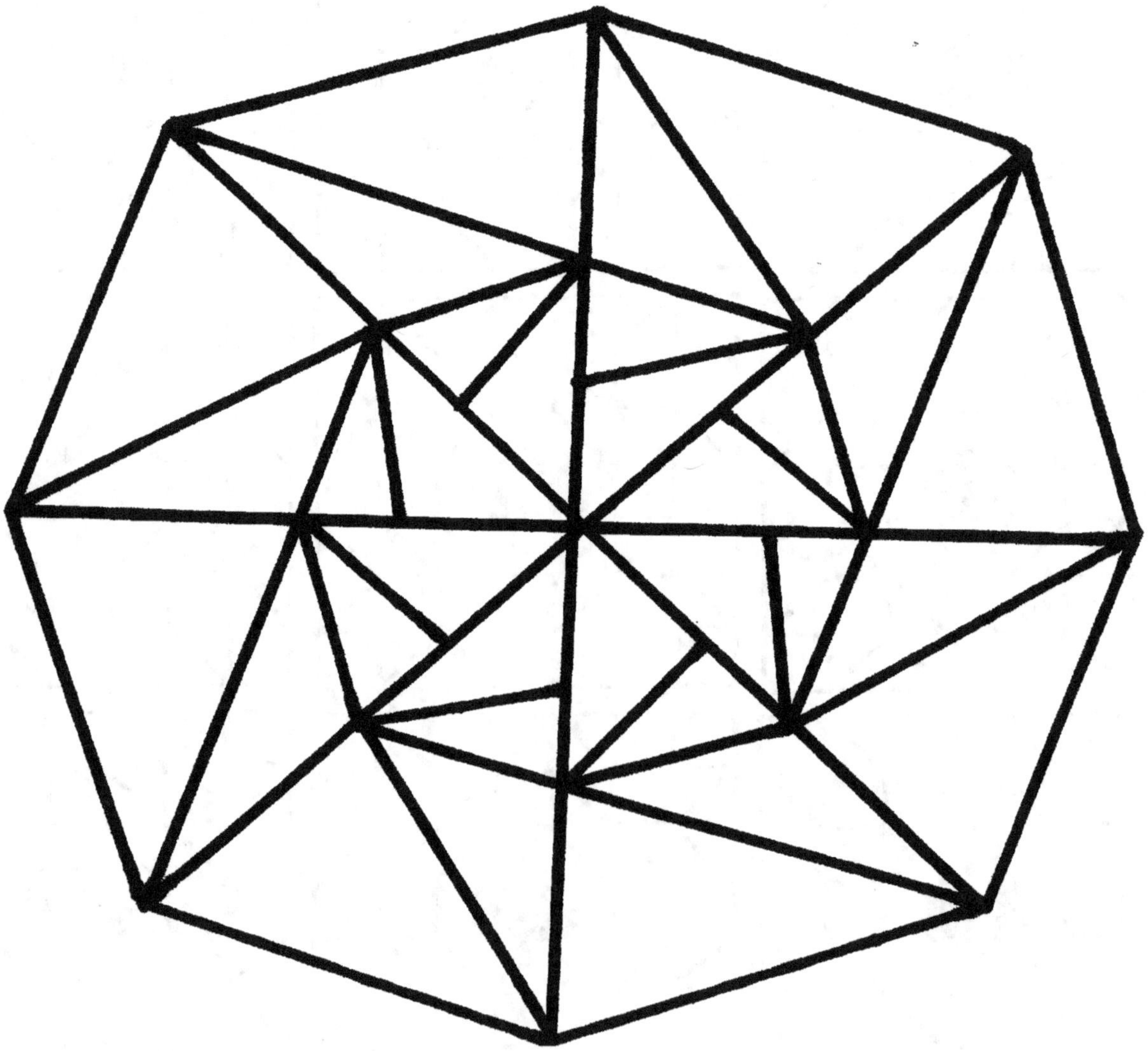

# Wisconsin Barn Quilt Joseph's Coat

# Always in Tune

## Shawano County Wisconsin Barn Quilts

*Barn Location*
*County rd K*
*Shawano, Wisconsin*

# Wisconsin Barn Quilt Always in Tune

# Let Freedom Ring

## Shawano County Wisconsin Barn Quilts

*Barn Location*
*County Trunk CC*
*Shawano, Wisconsin*

# Wisconsin Barn Quilt Let Freedom Ring

# Game Farm

## Shawano County Wisconsin Barn Quilts

*Barn Location*
*J&H Rd*
*Shiocton, Wisconsin*

# Wisconsin Barn Quilt Game Farm

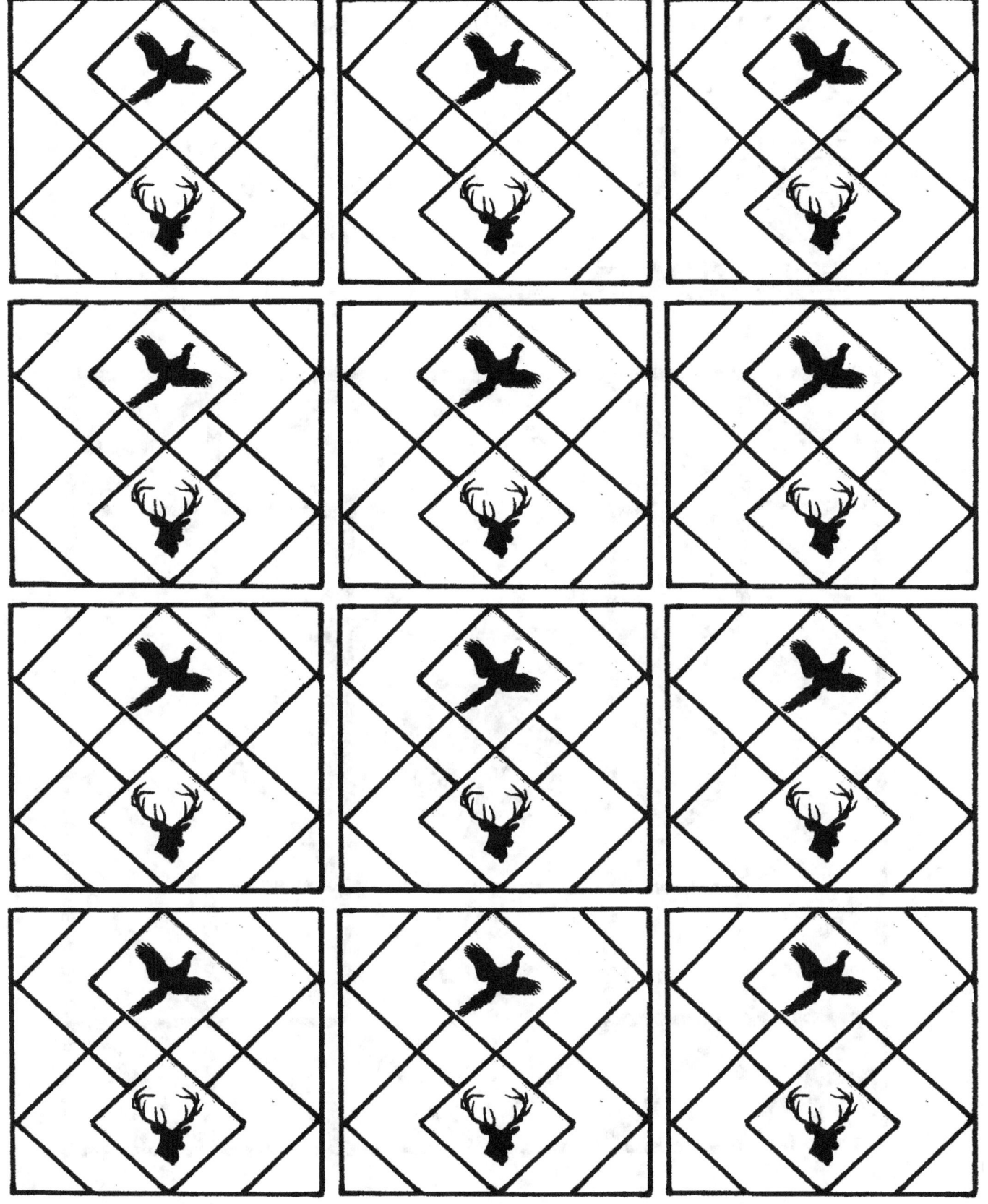

# Mosaic Squares
## Shawano County Wisconsin Barn Quilts

*Barn Location*
*Hwy 22*
*Shawano, Wisconsin*

# Wisconsin Barn Quilt Mosaic Square

# Victorian Star

## Shawano County Wisconsin Barn Quilts

*Barn Location*
*County Trunk CC*
*Shawano, Wisconsin*

# Wisconsin Barn Quilt Victorian Star

# The Wishing Horse
## Shawano County Wisconsin Barn Quilts

**Barn Location**
**County Rd C**
**Krakow, Wisconsin**

# Wisconsin Barn Quilt The Wishing Horse

# Wisconsin

## Shawano County Wisconsin Barn Quilts

*Barn Location*
*Hwy 22*
*Shawano, Wisconsin*

# Wisconsin Barn Quilt Wisconsin

# Norwegian Cross
## Shawano County Wiisconsin Barn Quilts

*Barn Location*
*Hwy 156*
*Shiocton, Wisconsin*

# Wisconsin Barn Quilt Norwegian Cross

# Castor and Pollux

### Shawano County Wisconsin Barn Quilts

*Barn Location*
*Wilson Creek Lane*
*Wittenberg, Wisconsin*

# Wisconsin Barn Quilt Castor & Pollux

# *Never Forget*

## *Shawano County Wisconsin Barn Quilts*

*Barn Location*
*Hwy 22*
*Cecil, Wisconsin*

# Wisconsin Barn Quilt Never Forget

# Family Traditions
## *Shawano County Wisconsin Barn Quilts*

*Barn Location*
*Deering Lane*
*Cecil, Wisconsin*

# Wisconsin Barn Quilt Family Traditions

# READING & MATH BOOKS by JOHN H. LETTAU

|  |  |
|---|---|
| 1st Dimension | Grades 3-6 |
| 2nd Dimension | Grades 3-6 |
| Primary Dimension | Grades 1-4 |
| | |
| Aztec Math Primary Book One | Grades 1-3 |
| Aztec Math Primary Book Two | Grades 1-3 |
| Aztec Math Intermediate Book One | Grades 3-6 |
| Aztec Math Intermediate Book Two | Grades 3-6 |
| | |
| Aztec Math Jr. High Book One | Grades 5-8 |
| Aztec Math Jr. High Book Two | Grades 5-8 |
| Aztec Math Decimal Book | Grades 4-8 |
| Aztec Math Fraction Book | Grades 4-8 |
| | |
| Sum-Action Number Puzzle Book One | Grades 3-6 |
| Sum-Action Number Puzzle Book Two | Grades 3-6 |
| Sum-Action Number Puzzle Primary Book One | Grades 1-3 |
| Sum-Action Number Puzzle Primary Book Two | Grades 1-3 |
| Multiplication Number Puzzles | Grades 3-6 |
| | |
| Geometric Design Puzzle Book One | Grades 3-6 |
| Geometric Design Puzzle Book Two | Grades 3-6 |
| | |
| Aztec Reading Primary Book One | Grades 1-3 |
| Aztec Reading Primary Book Two | Grades 1-3 |
| | |
| Math in Action | Grades 3-6 |
| A-Maze-ing Number Puzzles | Grades 3-6 |
| Graph Paper Designs | Grades 2-6 |
| Pick-A-Dilly Papers | Grades 3-6 |
| Awards for All Reasons | Grades 1-6 |
| Time Marches On | Grades 1-3 |
| Pennies, Nickels & Dimes | Grades 1-3 |
| Super-Sum Activity Cards | Grades 3-6 |
| Learning Center Game Boards | Grades 1-3 |
| Aztec Design Coloring Book | Grades 1-6 |

# *John Lettau Coloring Books*

## *Barn Quilt Coloring Books*

American Barn Quilt Coloring Book
Shawano County Wisconsin Barn Quilt Coloring Book One
Shawano County Wisconsin Barn Quilt Coloring Book Two
Shawano County Wisconsin Barn Quilt Coloring Book Three
Green County Wisconsin Barn Quilt Coloring Book
Delaware County Iowa Barn Quilt Coloring Book
Tennessee Appalachian Barn Quilt Trail Coloring Book One
Tennessee Appalachian Barn Quilt Trail Coloring Book Two
Franklin County Vermont Barn Quilt Coloring Book
Lake County California Barn Quilt Coloring Book
Graph Paper Design Coloring Book

## *Geometric Patterns*

Geometric Design Coloring Book 1
Geometric Design Coloring Book 2
Geometric Design Coloring Book 3
Geometric Design Coloring Book 4
Geometric Design Coloring Book 5

## *Graph Paper Designs*

Create Geometric Quilt Designs with Graph Paper Designs

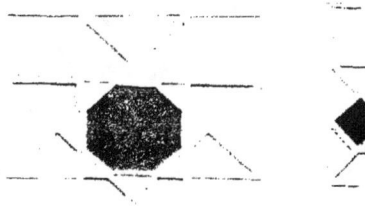 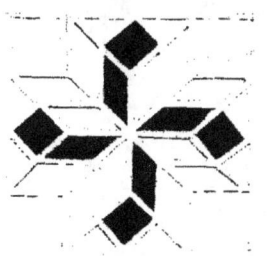 

**Color to Relieve Stress and Tension**

Order...John H. Lettau at Amazon.com